Pure Happiness

Awaken To Your Truth

Your Guide To Inner Freedom
Bob Molavi

To Alison,
great to meet you

with gratitude

This book is for those who went through their own 'dark night of the soul' and those who continue to go through their 'fire'. Know that I am with you on your journey.

Published by Neil and Cathy Schlosser

First Edition Printed June 2016
Second Edition Printed September 2016

Library and Archives Canada Cataloguing in Publication

Molavi, Bob, author

Pure Happiness: Awaken to Your Truth / Bob Molavi.

ISBN 978-0-9948468-2-2 (paperback)

1. Happiness. 2. Self-realization. I. Title.

BF575.H27M65 2016   152.4'2   C2016-903017-2

Feel free to contact the author for a presentation, to order books or any other information:
Bob Molavi, FMA, BA Econ
Happiness Coach

bob@purehappinesscoach.com
www.purehappinesscoach.com

Facebook: Bob Molavi / LinkedIn: Bob Molavi

Contents

Introduction 9

What is pure happiness? 13

The joy of winning... or is it? 16

If not now, when? 18

The need-to-win mentality 24

But don't we need goals? 28

So is it important to have "healthy" ego? 30

Mistake? What mistake? 34

Knowing thyself... 35

Who am I? 35

Fear factor 38

That was absolutely sensational! 41

Are our desires superficial? 42

Time to get deeper 45

Start with a beginner's mind 48

Be aware. Be very aware 49

Higher state of consciousness 52

Opening to life 56

Mindfulness 60

Head & shoulders 62

Need a new set of lenses?.............................63

Bumps along the way.....................................67

Your breath 68

Ohmmm! 71

Good vibrations...72

Yes! Yes! Yes! 73

Allowing...76

The BIG picture...78

Check your "gut" 81

Accumulation 84

Gratitude 84

Loving every minute..86

Money, money, money.....................................86

It's all relative 89

What's our highest currency?...........................90

Constant cravings 92

Nature or nurture...93

Remember the Jacksons? 95

Oh, and don't forget to SMILE :-) 97

About the Author...98

Acknowledgements 101

Introduction

The book you are about to read offers a different understanding of happiness as defined by the general public. It aims to expand your creativity, bolster your productivity, and deepen your relationship with life. Indeed, there is an abundance of get-rich motivational books laden with "feel good" information, equivalent to popping two white pills for temporary relief. But I am taking you on a different journey.

Many of the concepts you're about to digest are novel and somewhat counterintuitive. They are designed to trigger your deeper thoughts and aid you in discovering your own wisdom. There won't be much in terms of "ought" or "should", otherwise it wouldn't be self-discovery. Instead, the process you will be guided through will be visceral, concrete, and longer-lasting.

This book will align you with your true purpose and cleanse self-inflicted habits in the process. It will guide you in discovering the light within yourself instead of another. You will begin to see that the real search comes from within you, not out there.

Once this realization sets in, a transformation begins to take place. As you detox, your actions begin to take on a life of their own, coming more from your intuition, or inner wisdom rather than the gravitational pull of the masses. By deepening your authentic creative channel, there will be an outflow of a more natural you, and less dependency on external factors.

There is tremendous liberation in that.

This also means motivation won't be based on an outdated reward and punishment system, nor will it come by struggling and forcing you to do what you don't want to do.

Everybody seems to be searching for something. We seek a variety of methods to reach our goals, dreams, and overall fulfillment, yet it seems that regardless of the outcome, it's not good enough.

There are many motivational seminars, exotic trips, and expensive toys waiting to be experienced and enjoyed. We yearn for the stimulation of senses anywhere we can find it—a perpetual addiction to fulfill ourselves in every conceivable way—hungry for our next fix. One sensory experience begs to be followed by another. Whether from a psychological, scientific, spiritual, or economic perspective, it's an easy trap we fall prey to. These distractions are like a drug.

I believe you will find something completely different in this book from what you have been accustomed. It's very concentrated in format and packed with ideas that will help you in your life journey. There will be some perspectives that can be considered refreshers, but for the most part, the material thwarts what conventionally is taught as "success," particularly in a sales or business environment.

I won't spend pages of researched analysis, or throw together a bunch of theories hoping to convince you of ideas—that's already been done, plus it would take the fun out of it. Instead, you will discover for yourself what resonates.

When focusing inwardly, there is no guru sitting at the far corner of the earth who will offer you true liberation. If you are famous, wealthy, powerful, or gorgeous, it does not apply to your true happiness. The law of duality, to which mystics often refer, can readily pull you back in the opposite direction. The universe is keeping a ledger. Feelings of courage come with vulnerability. In order to understand tall, you must know short. Joy and peace are more aligned with our true nature.

For this journey, I'm here to help navigate through some roadblocks and personal barriers.

We'll be taking frequent breaks along the way. Oh, and you don't need to bring along any unnecessary baggage for this adventure—we'll be traveling light, so an open heart and mind, and a bit of music in your soul is all you really need.

The focus of this book is happiness, spirituality and freedom.

Eventually, we come to a point where the rubber meets the road. This is good. It gives us a chance to plant healthy seeds. From loving-kindness to stillness, we expand our hearts, aligning with true purpose where we surrender and let go—the gateway to our true purpose—to lighten our minds and deepen our souls.

I invite you to take this journey with me.

Let's begin.

What is pure happiness?

Right from the beginning, it's imperative that we define our pure happiness. Pure happiness is the kind of happiness that is inherent in your being. An academic, marketed, or articulate description has limitations.

The key point of pure happiness is a "state of equanimity" that goes beyond simple joys and pleasures. We know what it's like to feel great; the challenge is making it last. Pure happiness goes beyond commercialized happiness. It transcends what we normally describe as happiness.

Pleasure and pain are two sides of the same coin. If we pick up one side of the coin we pick up the other. Attempting to eliminate pain, we find, does not work and inevitably leads to suffering in one shape or another. So then the question becomes—is it possible to maintain this tranquil state, rather than hopping from one sensory pleasure to another? Can we find that place within us that we can finally call "home"?

The happiness that we seek is actually what moves us farther away from it. Upon further reflection, we find that what our soul is yearning for falls along the lines of a virtuous life rather than jumping from one instantly gratifying thing to the next. We've made massive strides in many areas to improve our lives—in medicine, technology, and science. We have a greater variety of food, nicer cars, and wall-sized TVs, yet it seems the more we have, the more we want, and the more unfulfilled we feel. Having things can make our lives more comfortable or easier and is not detrimental in itself, but it is the constant pursuit of wanting and craving which takes us further away from the conscious level.

I think right from the beginning, it's imperative that we focus on what our higher self wants, rather than what we think we want. A great way to start is by finding our truth instead of chasing happiness, which is what a majority of us in the West tend to do.

"Who looks outside, dreams. Who looks inside, awakes." – Carl Jung

"Happiness depends more on the inward disposition of mind than on outward circumstances." – Benjamin Franklin

This is what most of us tend to do in our daily lives. Seeking out there, when what we really should be doing, if we want to maximize our energy, is start from within.

The wealthy, famous, or powerful can feel depressed and miserable. There's a strong correlation between having more, but feeling less.

To get a more accurate reflection, there's also a GNH (Gross National Happiness), a formal indicator conceived by the government in Bhutan to measure happiness. Bhutan is a speck of a country squeezed within the geographical giants China and India. Citizens of Bhutan can teach us in many ways.

On the Bhutan Foundation website, there's a great quote: *"All happiness in the world arises out of wanting happiness for others." – Shantideva, 8th century*

In our culture, we've been conditioned to think that life is way too short, and the more experiences we have—more fame, power, health, and wealth we have, the happier we are. "Living it up" has become a cultural statement, and let's face it, it's tough not to buy into the system.

We really want to take a fresh, unbiased stance—stimulating and reprogramming the way we have been approaching life, and viewing it from the inside out.

"You attract and manifest whatever corresponds to your inner state." – Eckhart Tolle

Pure happiness has great ways of soothing our hearts. This includes music which can be from any genre. Beatles' songs are great examples: "Let it Be", "All You Need is Love" and "Come Together". We also have modern songs like Pharrell William's, "Happy". These titles show the spiritual essence of the songs. Any music that touches your heart and resonates with your soul improves your inner state.

The joy of winning... or is it?

Our culture has its own version of the game of life. Essentially, in order to win, you play by societal rules. Learn from your peers, successful acquaintances, institutions, and educational systems; then get married, have 1.5 children, land a professional job, and you will have a shot at making it to the finish line. Top dollars with an executive title and full medical/dental plans, stock options, a comfortable home with a two-car garage, luxury vehicles—follow the system, and the world will be your oyster.

This is also a game where winner takes all. We are all Darwinians now, or so it seems—submerged into the ruthless arena of life, we've accepted this competitive field as a natural way of life in order to evolve and move up the ladder. We demand greener lawns, better titles and whiter teeth. The game requires showing our best poker face. As we make our way towards the top, it may involve decisions that require us to temporarily ignore our core values, which could include spending less time with the family, yelling at a subordinate, or withholding great ideas from a co-worker.

So let's say after all the sacrifice required in filling our dream, we become masters of our destiny standing proudly on top of the hill to stake our claim to glory.

Why do some Hollywood celebrities keep returning to rehab, committing suicide, or resorting to alcoholism? They have all the fame, fortune, beauty, and money that anyone could possibly want. Given the choice of either being a celebrity in Los Angeles or living in poverty in Nigeria, I'm guessing we'd all grab the next flight to Hollywood.

Yet, somewhere very deep inside us (perhaps way deep), we know there's no lasting value in what people claim is important. We owe it to ourselves to see what this amazing race is all about before devoting our lives and taking the plunge without really even understanding what we are plunging into.

There are professionals who provide great advice and guide us through our journey but they can only do so much. Sure, there may be value to what they provide, but unfortunately, most people turn to them for a quick fix. Psychologists may be successful in treating neurosis. They can help in particular cases like when it comes to easing some of the immediate problems, but can they help you become a happier person, not just temporarily, but fundamentally?

Brokers, if focused on protection of long-term capital, provide an invaluable service. But are they providing a temporary or permanent solution?

If not now, when?

We convince ourselves that life will be better after we complete a stage in our life, like getting married and having a baby. External influences, from both family and friends, may cause us to actually believe there is something wrong with us if we don't blend in by achieving these goals within a period of time.

"First I was dying to finish high school and start college.
And then I was dying to finish college and start working.
And then I was dying to marry and have children.
And then I was dying for my children to grow old enough for school so I could return to work.

And then I was dying to retire.
And now, I am dying...and suddenly I realize I
forgot to live." – Unknown

How many people can you name who most probably fall under this category? Perhaps you've even been caught in a similar pattern.

So, if we have been so adamant in following the system we've been taught, and if we have narrowed ourselves to one of the lucky ones, why do we still feel this emptiness inside?

The great news is we can break this pattern any time we choose. Of course, it does require us to pay much closer attention to our actions than we have in the past. Not like the latest fitness program or New Year's resolutions but an inward transformation.

"Sing like no one's listening, love like you've never been hurt, dance like nobody's watching, and live like it's heaven on earth." – Mark Twain

"Insanity: doing the same thing over and over again and expecting different results." – Albert Einstein

"The object of life is not to be on the side of the majority, but to escape finding oneself in the ranks of the insane." – Marcus Aurelius

Some call it "going beyond your comfort zone" but here we are referring more to changing set patterns. We observe our own actions so that we can be the navigator of our lives, rather than our lives controlling us.

There's a Zen story of a man on a fast horse who seems to be going somewhere important. When a friend on the side of the road asks where he is going, the rider responds, "I don't know, ask the horse."

The more we are drawn into life's drama, the more helpless we feel and the more we tend to speed up. We become so engrossed with multitasking that we lose sight of our true purpose. We think we are moving ahead by doing more, whereas, on a larger scale, we are shrinking.

There comes a point where we're ostensibly holding the reins, no longer in control. If we look deeper on an absolute level most of us fall into the "ranks of the insane". We keep going through the same daily routine, running around keeping busy, putting out fires. This quickly turns into weeks, months, and years.

In *7 Habits of Highly Successful People*, Steven Covey talks about our society being addicted to urgency rather than efficiency. Having been directly involved in sales most of my life, I remember other staff racing around with intense looks, living on the edge. I would feel their frantic energy and get sucked into it. It was difficult not to.

Existing in this kind of environment feels like a loaded pistol pointed at your head. In my industry, I was exposed to many Type-A personalities— stressed out and resolute on their mission— briefcases in their hand and the weight of the world on their shoulders. It didn't take long to realize that being relaxed in this environment not only looked unnatural, but it felt unnatural too. During those times, where it was possible to catch your breath for a moment, guilt would set in. I thought, "If I really wanted success I'd better kick it up about seven notches."

One of my first jobs after university was for Accounts Payable at an energy pipeline company. My job was essentially to clear as many invoices as possible that landed on my desk. It was so overwhelming that the brief periods of time where the invoices slowed down, there was a feeling of complete relief—until the next day when bundles of more invoices would pile up in my inbox. The mini-breaks of relief were artificial fulfillment. The reward essentially wasn't an actual reward, but compared to the pain, it sure felt like one.

A good friend of mine worked at a communications company for many years. She told me about her stressful surroundings and late nights. Feeling miserable, but further masking it by being even busier, many staff ended up with health problems. Yet people would continue going through the grind.

We develop our own ways of coping with the grind, but eventually it gets to us.

In his book, The *Lazy Person's Guide to Success*, best-selling author Ernie Zelinski says that the longer some people are unhappy in a career, the more they feel comfortable being unhappy. It's analogous to an abusive relationship where people wonder how a spouse could stay with the other so long. We are more than just our jobs. We know that but tend to follow our programming out of fear of falling behind, not being competitive, or looking bad in front of our peers, who are pulling their weight.

For many others, it's also a matter of identifying with their job to the point where they feel anxious without it. Quite a paradox indeed!

You may recall a movie with Jack Nicholson, "About Schmidt". Essentially after his retirement farewell party, he went completely nuts—and no one does nuts quite like Jack! He offered to go back to work for free to see if anyone needed a hand but was sent back home. He began to reflect on his home, his life, and his wife. During one scene, he gets up in the middle of the night and looks at his wife, wondering, "Who is this old woman"?

If taking a five-minute break makes one feel guilty and unnatural, it may be a sign that one is a workaholic. If a frantic looking co-worker claims they can't remember the last time they sat down for lunch, it may be a sign they are a workaholic. The rare time they are still, they don't realize they're not taking advantage of that off-time because their minds and bodies are still thinking about work.

Are you one of those people who think about work when you're at home? If you want to become more productive at work, do both yourself and your boss a favor and use this time wisely to recuperate.

"Life is too short to be in a hurry." - Thoreau

"Life is what happens while you are busy making other plans." - John Lennon

In struggling to make ends meet, will completing challenging tasks feel rewarding to us? In most cases, it comes at a higher cost. Are we the equivalent of industrial chimney stacks, pumping out dark smoke when a cheaper, more environmentally responsible method is available? It's important to ask ourselves if we are poisoning and polluting our trails because eventually, it will catch up to us mentally, physically and emotionally.

This is all part of our cultural mandate—winners are rewarded. Too much emphasis is placed here. In being true to readers, and at the enormous risk of sounding like an outdated hippie, this is an area too important to neglect. It also defies what we have been taught.

How can one be successful without the need-to-win mentality?

Sales managers, coaches, and parents want winners. People want to be around other winners.

"We are the champions. No time for losers." - Queen

"Winning isn't everything, it's the only thing." - Green Bay Packers coach, Vince Lombardi

This is not only true in sports, but in everything we do in life. Let's face it, there is a thrill in winning. It's exciting. It's dramatic. As the judges on American Idol emphasized to the contestants, "Remember, you need to believe you can win."

Ah yes ... we love competition. We are taught to be champions from a very early age. In school, there is often a feeling of conditional love that's reserved for children who get the best grades and outrank their peers. The competitive drive transcends beyond the classroom in everything from sports to debates to video games.

From Roman gladiators to reality shows, we thrive on witnessing and experiencing the glory of winning and desperation of losing. Violence is craftily packaged as entertainment. Now soccer moms have even gotten into the ring to duke it out.

Remember for each winning team, there's a losing team. We are programmed to feel levels of inadequacy after a loss, or mock the other team. How much energy is exerted in winning and losing? And is that the best use of that energy? Now I'm certainly not advocating avoiding sports; it's a very healthy part of our lives. The difference is in how we choose to play.

Nowadays, working hard isn't good enough. You need to push harder. "Harder, Better, Faster, Stronger", as the song goes. We're looking for a better occupation, a faster car, a voluptuous body.

We have focused so much on outdoing others that we lose sight of what really matters.

There's got to be a better way.

"I'd rather be a failure at something I love than a success at something I hate."— Woody Allen

Does winning translate to happiness? Is winning really as important as we establish it to be?

What if we focused on the last two words—to be?

When we focus more on our being and less on external factors such as winning, we become more relaxed, and even more productive and effective! The need to win leeches your energy and focus and prevents you from actually enjoying the task at hand.

Various experts from Steve Jobs to Mihaly Csikszentmihalyi , say that when you become immersed in your task without external pressures, then enthusiasm and joy will accelerate your success whether you want it to or not!

Winning implies struggle. Struggle implies stress— the stress of needing to get ahead, which tips the scales towards the ego and less towards the soul.

Instead of a talent judge reminding the contestants they need to feel they are better than others, it would be refreshing to see that judge ask something that relates more to their passion. Instead, it's more about the glory of the win.

In *The Contrarian Effect* by Michael Port and Elizabeth Marshall, the authors mention that although the captain of the Titanic had a great deal of previous experience, his priority on that disastrous day was to beat the record of another large ship, the Olympus. In doing so, he missed all the warning signs because his mind was set on beating a record.

Why not challenge a system that preys on the misery of others instead? In sports, for example, we can train our kids to not focus so much on the win, the sweet taste of victory, but rather on the fun of the game.

One of my best friends had a great solution for the stress he felt while partaking in a hobby—in his case, golf. He talked about the added pressures that sometimes come with keeping score. He tried something different and hasn't looked back since. He doesn't use scorecards!

As a result, he had more energy and felt more enjoyment playing the game than he did when he treated it like a competitive sport. The paradox, of course, is now that he enjoys playing the game, his game has improved!

"The soft overcomes the hard; the weak overcomes the strong." - Lao Tzu

But don't we need goals?

"A good traveler has no fixed plans, and is not intent on arriving." - Lao Tzu

There is that great temporary feeling of accomplishment after reaching a goal, but if we allow that feeling to define us, hoping to recreate it again and again, we're bound to feel disappointment. Not only because we have to keep raising the bar to experience the same exuberance but also because the will to win was egoic (e.g. focused on beating the competition instead of mastering your talent) and so much of that energy could have been valuable in other ways.

Part of the winners' mentality involves setting goals. Goals should not be the goal. I realize this sounds almost ludicrous. Admittedly, even I have trouble rereading that sentence. We're not accustomed to seeing goals emphasized in most sales or business books.

Most business, sales, and motivational goals focus on the end result. But what if motivation can come from the process instead of just the result?
So far, we've been talking about some of the inherent problems in the way we've been doing

things. What if we were to find out what feels natural and true to ourselves?

When we set a goal and put all our energy towards it, we move towards the future. The business world would say we need this self-imposed pressure in order to stay motivated. In other words, effort or discipline is required. However, this again leads us to the conventional "no pain, no gain" mentality. As Krishnamurti said in one of his talks on PBS, "To be disciplined means to learn rather than conform."

Conforming keeps us from acting fully present. What if we could move goals aside so they're in our periphery so that we can focus more on the task at hand rather than reaching a set benchmark?

Eckhart Tolle suggests that goals imply working towards an end rather than the means to an end. In his book, *Power of Intention*, the late Dr. Wayne Dyer asks us to connect to this omnipresent force called intention; not as something you do, but as an energy you are part of. It's understandable that for most in our culture, this sounds counterintuitive. Intention is normally equated with struggling, paying your dues, no pain—no gain.

There is overwhelming medical and psychological evidence that indicates a host of illnesses are associated with stress. If stress is a cost of achieving our desired goal, will that goal make us happy? Are we the equivalent of racing Greyhounds, chasing a fake rabbit around a track, or is there a better alternative?

Tolle reminds us not to be concerned with the fruits of our actions but to pay attention to the action itself. Rather than relying on the toxic push to reach your goals, you should push yourself to search within and find deeper joy.

"The significant problems we face cannot be solved at the same level of thinking we were at when we created them." – Einstein

So is it important to have "healthy" ego?

Whether it's Vancouver's Robson Street, Calgary's Red Mile, or Toronto's Yorkville, on a summer evening, many enjoy dressing up the road with their freshly waxed sports car. You can hear the noise of engines revving, tires squealing and music thumping. It's a fashion show of sorts, and can be quite entertaining.

Upon closer examination, you could almost feel the pride and glory of the drivers—either to impress or race or simply get a date. I'll be the first to say, there's certainly no harm in enjoying fun-filled activities. It's more problematic when you depend on these outside influences to feel happier. The ego wants to be recognized. It is competitive, striving to win at all costs—it hates defeat. Ego loves to accumulate. Ego wants to impress and surpass others by feeling superior in some way. It wants to beat its chest and yell, "Victory!"

The ego is dialed into the copycat society.

"Be a first rate version of yourself, not a second rate version of someone else." – Judy Garland

"Your time is limited, so don't waste it living someone else's life." – Steve Jobs

While it's certainly helpful following role models who inspire us, we have to be extremely careful as to who we choose as role models. Advertisers are very good at picking up on this and take full advantage of fans who dream of becoming the next Justin Bieber. The logic then is: if I want to be, look, and talk like him, I should copy everything he's doing—and voila, we've got another copycat.

There's a fine line between respecting and worshipping. A person who starts worshipping spends more energy mimicking someone else than strengthening their own soul. Remember, all participants of life are given a different script. It's important that we follow our own. Otherwise, we fall into the trap of what Krishnamurti described as "second-hand human beings".

We probably know a number of successful people who have reached this point, yet continue doing what they do, not because of the money or the glory. There's only so much traveling you can do and caviar you can eat before the law of diminishing returns kicks in.

When the ego seeds are watered constantly, it grows into a monstrosity. That is why it is so important for overly ambitious people to do anything they can in their day to create space.

The ego assumes that everything you do is through you. That it is solely "you" that is creator of your talent and wants to be recognized as such. However, a healthy ego is an unhealthy life.

The ego is focused on greatness. But its definition of greatness is based on fame and fortune—the illusory aspects of life that distances itself from the soul.

The ego needs respect to fuel itself. On the surface, if one has reached a certain level, they may get that. But without a proper core, how authentic is the so-called "respect"? Here's a litmus test: If you lose your status, grow a potbelly, or go bankrupt, how many people in your life will stick around?

Joseph Campbell said, "Hell is being stuck in ego." It's a compulsive momentum that keeps us in fear.

We're all visionaries until we erect our own wall (ego), which becomes our reality. Some egos grow to such a scale that some people should have warning signs planted on their forehead like side-mirrors.

Warning: Suspects in life can be larger than they appear. Ultimately, ego is form based, an illusion projected from our minds. It creates the heaviness and drains our energy source.

One way to define ego is that it is an illusion of everything we think we are but actually aren't. Egos start to become self-defeating when they take over the "I". It starts as soon as we identify ourselves with our names, status, or countries.

The other drawback to ego is that it's the driving force that wants us not only to be perfect but to be perfect more quickly.

Of course, this is exactly what causes us to burn out in many of the ways discussed. It's unnatural, but it's common.

Another ego litmus test is to ask yourself: Do you desire to have, or do you prefer to be?

Freedom comes through when ego melts away. Freedom is where happiness, joy and peace reside.

Mistake? What mistake?

There is no shame in mistakes; after all, to err is human. We hear this often enough, but we still punish ourselves when we falter. This is an example of societal conditioning that does far more harm than good.

If we look closer at this, from a conscious level, we see that those mistakes were necessary in order for us to evolve.

Any worthwhile accomplishment had its share of time and dedication. Many are familiar with Thomas Edison's comment on failure: "I have not failed. I've just found 10,000 ways that won't work."

When we accept our mistakes it becomes part of our growth.

Knowing thyself...

"To be yourself in a world that is constantly trying to make you something else is the greatest accomplishment." —Ralph Waldo Emerson

It's hard to dispute the wisdom of Aristotle or the Dalai Lama who say that our purpose in life is happiness. If we look at the underlying motive in pretty much anything we do, we are ultimately seeking pleasure and avoiding pain. We can transcend this approach by simply growing the seeds of compassion into our lives.

Who am I?

In Self-Inquiry, who you are is basically thoughts, emotions or sense perceptions. This is how most of us see our world. Self-Inquiry broadens our scope so it is not as limited in the confines of the ego. Our egos prefer to stay in the dream, really the illusion or delusion. But we love the game so we continue with virtual reality—the colorful duality of feeling happy and unhappy with the ups and downs. We can pamper and massage our egos for days, years or lifetimes.

Many are familiar with the popular saying, "When the student is ready, the teacher will appear". When we have come to surrendering, which is an act of courage, not defeat, it allows for an internal expansion. Grace can then come through.

Einstein mentioned that we should look for what is and not for what we think should be.

Another way of approaching this is, "I AM". "Who am I?" goes well beyond consciousness and identity. It invites us to look into our true nature, beyond the person with the personality. It leapfrogs the mind and into the heart—a place of stillness. Interestingly, most spiritual books start off with a key message: You are not your mind.

I found in many workshops and gatherings, when I raise this topic, it brings an inquisitive look from the audience. This is a great opportunity for people to see for themselves, that if they personally decide to stop thinking, thoughts will start coming in automatically. This is one way of approaching the stillness of our mind.

"What lies behind us, and what lies before us are tiny matters compared to what lies within us." - Ralph Waldo Emerson

If you go beyond the glamour, power, prestige, and wealth, you might see an empty soul. The more this soul is fed with these "outside-in" distractions, the more it drowns in its own misery.

Jesus said, *"The greatest among you ought to be servant of all."* (Mark 10.43-44). For the masses still programmed by their egos, this is a very challenging barrier to overcome.

Once the real you is able to penetrate through the egoic barrier, a whole new world awaits. This requires a devotion to moving inward, and it requires humility.

David Hawkins, MD, Ph.D., wrote a number of books integrating science and spirituality. In *Discovery of the Presence of God*, he talks about humility being essential to spiritual growth and the ego's incapability of distinguishing truth from false. He goes on to talk about how our spirit is oriented towards context rather than content.

Again, scientists and sages, or those who are considered both, like Hawkins or Chopra, arrived at the same conclusions: that there is more to understanding life than just relying on content. It is my belief that content is limited to knowledge, but context is where wisdom is found.

"Be the change you want to see in the world." – *Gandhi*

While Self-Inquiry is permeating our soul, it becomes a magnet for others—a powerful contribution to humanity. When there's no inner pollution, we become more conscious of the world. We create and we provide relief for others. "Who am I?" and "I AM" continue to nourish our spirituality.

Fear factor

'If you are distressed by anything external, the pain is not due to the thing itself, but to your estimate of it; and this you have the power to revoke at any moment." – Marcus Aurelius

"The only thing we have to fear is fear itself." – FDR's first inaugural address

"As we are liberated from our own fear, our presence automatically liberates others." – Nelson Mandela

In addition to being a competitive society, we place a lot of emphasis on security. This creates fear. There is no shortage of things to be fearful of, whether it's poverty, sickness, or another oil spill. Many of us shove these fears to the back of our subconscious minds, like dirty socks in a suitcase.

But eventually, the problem escalates, leading to a host of self-destructive behaviors, like depression or anger.

Our culture operates on a mentality of fear rather than an abundance mentality. Fear creates mistrust and fuels the ego. It puts up barriers. Fear is a corrupt motivator. As soon as you feed it, there's a possibility of achieving whatever state of mind would have led you to avoiding fear in the first place, but at a much greater cost. I would definitely replace the seed of fear with another seed that directs you towards happiness.

"Do not anticipate trouble or worry about what may never happen. Keep in the sunlight." – Benjamin Franklin

Franklin's quote is a great reminder of how to burn through fear by staying in the present. There are many forms of fear. For example, fear can lead to ruthlessness. Society has trained us to view ruthlessness as a noble trait. People like Stalin saw ruthlessness as a virtue. Other historical figures like Genghis Khan, Hitler, or Saddam were part of this elite group.

However, fear cultivates seeds of darkness, and the individual (and his victims) suffer as a result. Even if ruthlessness defeats the enemy, it creates distrust and isolation and eventually suffering. If people draw their strength from fear rather than compassion, ruthlessness grows.

Compassion is a tenet of Buddhist philosophy. The Dalai Lama describes it as a wish for others to be free of their suffering. Cultivating compassion provides so many benefits that it's difficult to know where to start. Not only does it provide the obvious benefit of making others feel good, but it fast tracks you to happiness (so even selfish people have a compelling reason to jump on this train).

When recovering from surgery, I remember the desire to feel more compassion. I started sending silent blessings out to strangers. Over at the coffee shop, despite my grim financial situation, I bought strangers coffee without them knowing who paid. After such experiences, I felt quite alive and content.

I remember not too long ago, around Christmas, there was a huge article in the newspaper providing research confirming something we've long been told—that giving provides greater satisfaction than receiving. I don't think we have to rely on such research to be convinced of taking compassionate action. We can be our own researchers and experience the results first-hand.

That was absolutely sensational!

If you really think about it, we live in a culture of sensation seekers scurrying from one stimulating activity to another. Buddhism talks about "samsara", or the wheel of suffering. It's a hopeless cycle for those thinking they can find consistent pleasure and avoid pain.

There is only so much one can do to entertain oneself. We talked about the law of diminishing returns earlier, where you require escalating amounts of pleasure in whatever form until it can no longer be attained. This creates a vicious cycle where we eventually have to pay the price.

Without getting lost in semantics, I will define pure happiness here as a more permanent state that, as Rumi described, is like a river flowing within you, a joy. Most people confuse happiness with pleasure. They are locked in samsara, chasing the next sensation and not realizing it's a double-edged sword.

Short-term relief creates a long-term problem if one is attached to the experience.

Are our desires superficial?

Desire itself implies attachment, which implies getting caught in the wheel of samsara. Most of us have experienced walking into a fast-food place, enjoying biting into a greasy, juicy burger, only to feel uncomfortable a few hours later. This isn't to suggest abandoning all necessary evils, just being aware of your activities and keeping a balance that feels right.

I recall having a casual conversation at a club with a real-estate agent—we'll call him John. After a few beverages, John confessed that although he was very successful with the ladies, after a series of conquests, he was left feeling this great sadness. He said he felt like absolute crap for about a week. A creature of habit, he would continue a similar pattern the following Friday.

In his bestselling book, *Stumbling on Happiness*, psychologist Daniel Gilbert emphasized that people are bad predictors of what makes them happy. I would add that most of these approaches are targeted towards pleasure, neglecting the laws of samsara.

Between moments of pleasure, we are required to pay a price. Even in chaos, there is a perfect order. But don't take my word for it. Next time when experiencing a pleasurable moment, bring your practice of awareness to the activity. Bring your awareness with complete focus and energy.

To pull out of the samsara trap we were discussing earlier, it's not necessary to avoid those activities that provide pleasure. There is a very important distinction, and that is "to be in the moment". Not to be attached to either the pain or pleasure, but allow it to flow through sensing its arrival, like a welcome guest.

If you are able to practice moving into the present moment, then you have received more value than perhaps anything else. It's worth far more than fame, money, or power—and by a long shot.

Pleasure and pain are transitory. The treasure we look for is buried within.

"You can't always get what you want, but if you try sometime, you find you get what you need." - The Rolling Stones

"When I let go of what I am, I become what I might be. When I let go of what I have, I receive what I need." - The Tao Te Ching

Another time I was visiting a friend back East who lived a very comfortable and luxurious life. He was healthy, drove high-end cars, frequented high-end restaurants, and spent time with friends. But he always seemed empty. His eyes were hollow, and he always seemed to be searching for some kind of relief, some kind of meaning.

Fame, power, or fortune is merely an artificial sweetener. And the more you have, the more you expand your sweet tooth, perpetuating a vicious cycle. It's like trying to find meaning through unnatural means, creating a cavity and leaving you feeling painful and hollow. This is similar to the movie "CRASH".

One of the central messages of the film is that people are so lonely and wanting to validate their existence that they are unconsciously setting themselves up for an accident just to be able to connect with somebody.

Remember, living from, rather than for happiness, is the basis of insight. That dangling carrot of samsara may only show you the pleasurable side, but realize its opposite is around the corner.

"There are only two tragedies in life: one is not getting what one wants, and the other is getting it."
– Oscar Wilde

Perhaps you win the lottery, start working out and building the perfect body, or are surrounded by twelve lovely maidens feeding you grapes. Initially, it would probably feel like you're living a fantasy. But reality is always waiting around the corner. Avoid hopping on the samsara wheel.

Time to get deeper

"I want to know God's thoughts; the rest are details." – Einstein

"Happiness comes from spiritual wealth, not material wealth; from giving, not getting. If we try hard to bring happiness to others, we can't stop it from coming to us. To get joy, we must give it, and to keep joy, we must scatter it." – John Templeton

Whether one is religious, atheist, or agnostic, the philosophical differences aren't as great as we may think. Most physicists agree that there is a connective or universal force at play. This is the force that coordinates the flow of synchronistic events—everything from migrating birds to the coordination of a 100 trillion cells, with each cell acting as a microcomputer in each human body.

There's a misconception that faith in a higher source, whether it's God, Buddha or Allah, falls under the domain of less intelligent people. If intelligence is derived from collecting information as well as personal experience, how far can it go?

It may advance us in our careers or be a great source of reference.

What we see is not just based on our intelligence; it goes beyond this. It requires wisdom—wisdom meaning going beyond the mind. This is Self Inquiry From The Heart.

Self-Inquiry is the core of spirituality. It begins to offer some of the benefits as soon as you start practicing. Although I'm sure it makes for a great experience, Tolle, and other enlightened individuals remind us that it's not necessary to join a monastery, an ashram or seek a guru.

When the student is ready, the teacher will appear. Contemporary teachers like Deepak Chopra and Wayne Dyer have reminded us that we are not humans having a spiritual experience, but rather spirits having a human experience. When we begin to start recognizing that we are in this world and not of it, there becomes a sense of lightness and buoyancy. Life no longer needs to be taken so seriously and we start being more ourselves.

Seeking the meaning of life, the ability to recognize that there's something out there much larger than us, has allowed humanity to evolve. Socrates once asked why people care so much about things like money, honor, and reputation, yet so little about truth and improving the soul.

Thinkers, both ancient and contemporary, including Plato, Maharishi, Emerson and Jung understood the need to go beyond mere thought to true connection with a larger source.

This, of course, involves living with an open heart and curious mind. We have been so conditioned throughout our lives to care about what others think, to follow their success principles or resort to dogma, that we forgot to really be ourselves. In the process, the mind atrophies, and in its place, cravings have a stronger hold.

Where we can begin to expand is being willing to move beyond copycatting and dogma. There's a reason why sages were only able to help us so much. After that, life is designed to be a journey of self-inquiry.

As Jesus said, "Seek and you shall find." (Matthew 7.7)

Buddha said, "The truth is like the moon, and all of my teachings are like the finger pointing at the moon."

Much teaching is limited to words, which is often misconstrued for objective reality.

A great part of what pulls us away from our true selves is comparing ourselves to others. Many times we do this unconsciously and it gets us into trouble. This comparison game has saturated our culture. Our sense of self is continuously challenged by what others are doing. It's very difficult to pull away from how we've been raised to think.

Start with a beginner's mind

"In the beginner's mind there are many possibilities, but in the expert's there are few." – Shunryu Suzuki, Zen Mind, Beginner's Mind

Shoshin means beginner's mind. The goal is to keep an empty and ready mind. This keeps us fresh, agile, and creative. It will open up more doors you otherwise wouldn't have had since most of us are so easily caught in routine.

As I was going through a personal transformation, I noticed my habits changing. The type of music I'd listen to would be softer. In fact, when I would drive, I was listening to the radio less often—not because I wanted to develop any specific kind of habit, but because I found the quiet extremely soothing.

Sometimes the best sound in the world is silence.

Be aware. Be very aware.

"By giving your full attention to this moment, an intelligence far greater than the egoic mind enters your life." – Eckhart Tolle, Stillness Speaks

Being aware means being fully present. Right this second.

A key Zen message is to give the present moment our fullest attention. We are so immersed in the past and future that we forget the most important thing in our lives—NOW.

"BE-ing" sums up many spiritual teachings, increases concentration, and dramatically enhances our quality of life. When it comes to the economics of life, the art of being is the biggest bang for your buck.

One of Canada's largest telecommunications companies, Telus, has the slogan, "The future is friendly." I'd like to add a small twist: the present is friendlier.

We are so occupied with moving onto the next thing that we neglect the moment: the taste of tea; the feel of a breeze against our skin; our breath as we inhale and exhale.

Of course, keeping our focus on the moment is much easier said than done. We tend to be consumed by our past or future. Although there is nothing wrong with this in itself, it takes us away from life's precious gift. There is a reason it's referred to as the "present".

When you're friendly with the present, your actions are no longer reactionary. You go beyond the clutches of stimulus and response, by-passing psychologist B.F Skinner's example of reward and punishment.

Woody Allen once quipped that 80 percent of success was showing up. If you show up consciously, then you're up to 100 percent.

By being in the moment, we also remind ourselves that it is the journey and not the destination that is important. When we have a WHY, then the HOW becomes a formality. Most of us have the destination or goal as the main focus and being present as secondary when it should be the other way around.

Sometimes it is more challenging to be present while watching exciting movies. We know the feeling we get when we are sitting at the edge of our seat at the movie theater with our eyeballs glued to the big screen. Popular movies, often action ones, have plots in which the protagonist faces some enemy, has his ego bruised, and eventually seeks his revenge. The viewer equates justice with payback.

Although this is merely entertainment, it's important not to nurture the wrong seeds when trying to harvest an organic mind. The temporary high—like rushing to meet deadlines or having three shots of expresso—is often followed by the low.

Sure, the rush feels fantastic at first. But unless we are faced with immediate danger, our speedier heart rates, dilated pupils and tense muscles (essentially a fight-or-flight response) prematurely wears us down, creating its own vicious circle that requires more stimulation to overcome.

I've seen too many good people fall victim to this adrenaline trap to the point where it becomes their new normal. Our systems weren't designed for this. It's like being on code red when there's no imminent danger. Being in the present allows us to keep grounded.

Emerson said, "A man [or woman] is what he [or she] thinks about all day long."

Studies show we have 90,000 or more thoughts a day. That's a lot of thinking! Most of this thinking is recycled loops—the same things over and over again. In fact, the definition of insanity is repeating the same actions (or thoughts) but expecting different results. Sometimes we notice what we think, but most of the times we don't. We're stuck in either the past or future.

A busy person decides to take a vacation to get away from things. Even though they may be at some tropical Island enjoying Pina Coladas, for the most part their mind is wavering, calculating, locked in the past and future. Their attention is everywhere else but there. I loved Jon Kabat Zinn's example where he says at this point a person may as well send themselves a postcard saying, "Wish you were here."

Higher state of consciousness

Just as it's great practice to observe our thoughts, it's a bonus to watch the gaps within the thoughts—mini meditations. It's a great way to expand beyond the five senses.

At work, we are often taught to think, to keep thinking until it hurts. When we observe the thoughts and the gaps, with practice, we can still continue with our daily functions except this time, the conditioned mind isn't running the show. You are witnessing your mind.

Being the observer of our life acts as a virus-blocker of unwanted programming, slowing or infecting our system.

Whatever is stored in our bundled conditioning is normally what determines our response. Rather than our impulses taking over when someone cuts you off on the road, it's a good opportunity to test yourself. More often than not, it's not personal. But your negative reaction and bundled conditioning can ruin an entire day. It creates a domino effect of negative energy.

Research has shown that if we perceived to have had a negative experience prior to making a decision, it will influence how we make our next decision. So now, because someone cut you off, if your conditioning takes over, it sets off a chain reaction bringing on more of the same experiences. During the rest of your drive to work, you're less inclined to allow another driver to merge in front of you.

When you're revved up, it takes away from your mental and physical energy. It may increase the odds of spilling coffee on someone else.

The other option is to observe your reaction.

When you see that certain energy comes from a feeling, here's a chance to practice. What is this energy inside me? Does it feel like a flow or a craving? Does it make me feel empty inside? Does it spark rage and create aggression? This is the opportunity to meet the emotion head on and go deeper—take your surfboard and crash towards the wave of emotion. See how you feel.

There are a number of people who are fortunate enough to transcend their automated lifestyle to ask the fundamental question—What do I want out of life? If we want to go beyond this, an even better question to ask might be—What does life (God or universe) want out of me?

Once this question percolates in our minds, our direction begins to change. We now begin to connect more with our environment and with greater intensity. This alone is a great starting point. Normally, when we hear of cleansing, we relate it to our bodies, but we don't take it to the next level.

Cleansing of the mind is a bit different. It requires perseverance. It requires practicing awareness and surrendering to a more expansive reality. It seeps the air out of the ego balloon.

When we do so, we move towards equanimity, becoming more rooted and balanced. Reactive impulses naturally begin to lessen.

"Be a light unto yourself." – Buddha

Focusing on your own light may sound like a selfish action, but by focusing on compassion and love, you not only benefit yourself but more importantly, you benefit those you come in contact with. When you're angry at someone and their first inclination is to become defensive or angry in return, by expanding the light from within you, you pave the way for better communication. On a larger scale, you're fulfilling a noble purpose in life—you're leaving the world in a better place than you found it.

The wonderful thing about Buddhist teaching is that it's not really considered a religion but a way of life—a way of achieving lasting happiness. Many spiritual teachers such as the Dalai Lama or Jon Kabat-Zinn define Buddhism as a "training of the mind".

Not just the intellectual "mind", but the holistic mind, body and soul. I think the phrase "mind over matter" should be slightly adjusted to "no-mind", according to Buddhists. It's not just our thinking, but our Being, that navigates us. In our culture, we tend to take our minds for granted. In fact, we pay a lot more attention to our bodies and expect the mind to take care of itself.

However, mind and body work in conjunction. If you take care of one and ignore the other, you'll soon be faced with barriers.

In the *Art of Happiness*, the Dalai Lama and others, discuss research conducted on the part of the brain associated with happiness. When they compared the level of Buddhist monks to average Americans, not only was there a difference, it was OFF THE CHARTS. Here's another example of merging Eastern and Western practices where science and spirituality provide the same conclusion.

By learning to become more self-aware and train ourselves, we begin to create our own destiny on more favorable terms.

Opening to life

"Your vision will become clear only when you look into your heart. Who looks outside, dreams. Who looks inside, awakens." – Carl Jung

"Let yourself be silently drawn by the stronger pull of what you really love." – Rumi

Conventional teaching says that in order to become successful, you must sacrifice your present life for a better future. Here's another adage that must be taken with a grain of salt. The very word "sacrifice" implies an effort, some form of mental or physical pain to get from here to there.

Again, when we give our full effort towards a goal, there is the danger of needless stress, losing sight of the present moment, and distracting yourself from your deeper purpose. Your current situation is a means to an end. Perhaps you are successful at reaching the goal, but the added costs along the way are too steep to ignore. A more effective approach would be to focus more on the journey than the destination. That's one of the few clichés I could actually sink my teeth into.

A wonderful feeling of inner peace occurs when we become our own counselors. We become our own judge and jury.

Viktor Frankl was a Holocaust survivor and psychiatrist. His profound message was that everything can be taken from a person, except for one thing: freedom to choose under any set of circumstances. This is our greatest gift. The freedom to choose differentiates us from all the other animals.

It is this very right that provided Dr. Frankl true freedom even under the most heinous circumstances. There was a point in his book,

Man's Search for Meaning, where Frankl described how he was tempted to wake up other prisoners when they were having nightmares. But then he figured that the living nightmare of being in the concentration camp was probably worse than whatever they were dreaming.

If Frankl can recognize true freedom under those conditions, then all of us can.

We have the option to pull ourselves out of auto-pilot. Remember, if we don't shape our mind, it will begin to shape itself. The danger then becomes getting locked into the painful grip of life, chasing temporary pleasures but missing out on the real fruit. It would be acting from an unconscious state. The brain that fires together, wires together.

In order to appreciate this gift, to transcend from zombie status, there needs to be awareness. It sounds so simple. Wherever you are, be fully aware. Feel every sensation. Feel the air. Observe your environment without letting the stream of thinking take over.

Just be!

Giving our full attention is not as easy as it sounds. It sounds paradoxical by saying that in order to be mindful, we need to observe the emptiness of the mind. That's where we tap into a higher dimension of thought. Like any practice, this may appear challenging at first since we are addicted to immediate gratification and react through conditioned thought patterns.

A common example of this is our casual response to common greetings.

Often, people approach you and ask, "How are you?" We tend to respond by automatically saying, "Good."

On occasion, we bring in our heart as a guest, and make the slight change to, "How are you, really?"

This is not only from an engaged level but from a higher conscious level. It reminds us that we're not this little entity fighting our way through life; we are life itself. Who and what you are go beyond your mental habits. When we accept and surrender more to what we are not, we allow life to come through.

Grace can emanate joy, peace and equanimity. With this, our life becomes clearer and egoic gremlins disappear.

"We are what we repeatedly do. Excellence, then, is not an act, but a habit." - Aristotle

*"You can't live well in one depth of your life." –
Gandhi*

If you are a life coach in the day and kick your dog
when you come back home, chances are you will
have some alignments that require mending.
Remember, the universe keeps track, and you end
up creating your own suffering.

Mindfulness

Mindfulness, from a spiritual perspective, actually
means "no mind" as we talked about previously.
Instead of filling our minds up, we are emptying
them out. This is a way of bringing in more
awareness and less ego.

When we practice mindfulness, another great side
benefit is diminishing our negative habits. Like a
good investment fund, these newly formed habits
begin to generate compound interest for the soul.

Mindfulness is better than merely thinking. Eckhart
Tolle and Dr. Dennis Merritt Jones remind us of
the limitations of Descartes when he said, "I think,
therefore I am." We are not our thoughts, even
though we may think we are. A more accurate
statement would be "I am, therefore I think."
Understanding this deeper relationship takes us

out of stimulus/response and connects us deeper with our destiny.

A number of psychologists like Jung, Maslow and Csikszentmihalyi shared similar thoughts. Maslow said there was a connection between people who had outstanding creativity and strong character, and that was mystical experiences. This upset some of the psychology community as it strayed from linear thinking. The term was then replaced by what is commonly known as "peak experiences".

Spiritual teachings refer to an emptiness which is a portal in itself to understanding the meaning of life. Homer Simpson could have been onto something the producers didn't intend. When he wasn't busy thinking of donuts or Duff beer, there were gaps of emptiness. Wouldn't it have been interesting if, in the very last episode of the series, they disclosed that Homer was actually a Zen master?

By learning to become more aware or mindful of ourselves and our surroundings, we begin to notice a shift in the way we do things. It could be having less of a desire to watch violent movies, use less profanity, or eat less junk food. Whatever the case may be, our outer world begins to change accordingly. For every action, there is an opposite reaction. The harmony becomes noticeable and our quality of life begins to blossom.

When you are inspired, or in-spirit, you are more attuned to your surroundings. By being mentally naked, your intuition picks up on signals you otherwise wouldn't; similar to a blind person whose other senses are boosted to compensate for sight.

Being inspired also moves us deeper into self-awareness.

Every minute thought has enough potential to trigger a chain of events similar to the so-called "butterfly effect". What you think about and how you act determines your quality of life. This is why self-awareness is so important. "You are what you eat" applies to your mental state as well. You are what you think about. With right thinking, you don't leave a shadow.

"Your unhappiness ultimately arises not from the circumstances of your life, but from the conditioning of your mind." – Eckhart Tolle

Head & shoulders

When it comes to spirituality, scrubbing daily keeps us fresh.

We know how good it can feel after a shower. Similarly, when it comes to happiness and spirituality, we are able to scrub our mind and body, as we do in meditation.

In our Eckhart Tolle gatherings, when I start our mini-meditation, I remind participants to drop their shoulders. It's amazing how many keep their shoulders tense throughout the day, and instantly feel a deep release after a few seconds.

Ahhhhhhh!

With practice this becomes automatic.

Need a new set of lenses?

If you begin to really understand that you are a witness to your mind and not trapped inside it, you will see a dramatic improvement in your life. Of course, like anything else, this may not happen overnight. It takes diligence. Not in trying to achieve something, not setting ambitious targets and pushing the pedal to the metal, but by going deeper within.

Remember, we're handed different instruction manuals and the only one able to crack the code is you. This requires a bit of openness in the way we are used to doing things.

Wayne Dyer emphasized in his books that when you change the way you look at things, the things you look at change. Reprogramming our bundled conditioning by simply being aware of our actions gets the process started.

Recall that you are not your thoughts. We can catch ourselves repeating the same phrases, labeling or fault-finding. This is not just a mental disorder. According to physicists, it works its way into the body as well.

We make many decisions during the day. Being consciously aware at that moment takes us away from our mental loop. If the solution doesn't present itself, then we need to make a choice. In *The Art of Happiness*, the Dalai Lama provides an invaluable tip prior to making a decision: Will this decision provide me greater happiness or greater pleasure?

Although the two sound very similar, it usually results in two different outcomes. Most of us in Western culture go after the pleasure, after our cravings. However, hedonistic tendencies usually come at the expense of pure happiness.

After reading this, you will come to see there's a bit more to it. Both pleasure and sadness are a part of life. They are inevitable. Rather than focusing on the goal of happiness, it makes more sense to be in the present moment as much as possible. This pulls you out of the clutches of samsara.

To be able to appreciate the rollercoaster ride of life, feel free to just lift your arms up and let go. If you focus on living fully instead of seeking happiness, your life will be far more fulfilling.

Allowing for life to unfold opens us up to another dimension. When we are less concerned with how we compare, we create the foundation for integrity. Our activities will naturally become more loving, generous, and relaxed.

Rather than repeating the same flawed programs in our minds, it's worth having a closer examination of what we are actually thinking. Of course, this is far easier said than done and will require diligence. For example, gossiping, a popular verbal sport, is very potent. It's easy to get caught up in the drama. We temporarily feel vibrant and more alive. But it also sucks out our vital energy that can be used in a far more beneficial way.

For some reason, a conversation I had a couple decades ago didn't really sink in until much later. I started talking with a man in a lounge. He had an amazing aura about him. On the surface, he seemed at peace. He spoke in a calm manner and had a very natural smile.

During the course of the conversation, I asked him if he had seen a certain movie. I think it was a Tarantino blockbuster or something of the sort. He'd heard of it, but told me he is very cognizant of what he puts into his head. Sometimes you'll hear a simple comment that can alter the way you view life. This was one of those times. Although I watch the odd thriller or gory movie, I decided a while back to keep it to a minimum.

Aristotle's philosophical teaching discusses "virtue", which is equivalent to happiness.

Here again, is where it's helpful to watch our actions. Do we feel more alive when we watch breaking news, engage in gossip or walk through a Vegas strip mall? Or do we honor the situation without getting attached to it?

One mindful step at a time. One simple breath at a time.

Buddhist teaching provides a great analogy of our life as an ocean. Instead of thinking of the ripples as the meaning of your life, and getting caught up in the ripples, see the ocean underneath the surface.

"You are not a drop in the ocean. You are the entire ocean in a drop." – Rumi

Practicing these activities systematically removes our ego and brings us closer to our natural state.

Bumps along the way

"Be kind, for everyone you meet is fighting a hard battle." – Plato

"Hatred is never ended by hatred, but by love." – Buddha

In one of my blogs, I began with, "Life is difficult". These were the first words of Scott Peck's *The Road Less Travelled,* which became another all-time bestselling classic. Krishnamurti refers to life as a constant battle.

At times it seems we're the only ones dealing with hardship. There are many who feel they are stuck with problems no one else has. However, by digging below the surface, a different story usually emerges. Even the ones who seem to have It all seem to have the greatest challenges.

Your breath

Although a great title for a Listerine commercial, we're focusing here on something most of us hardly pay attention to.

Your breath is the foundation for everything else. Your lungs act automatically, 24/7, replenishing your cells on a second-per-second basis. If it stops functioning for even a brief moment, the organism (that means you) stops operating. Breathing is something we take for granted.

The best way to get into our "zone" is by noticing our breath. Focusing on your breath is a great relaxant. It is common practice to take a few deep breaths before heading into an important meeting, writing a big exam, or jumping out of a plane.

Sri Ramana Maharshi, the enlightened spiritual teacher, mentions a gently indrawn breath, with no thought, can bring total awareness.

Focusing on our breath has so many benefits. Not only does it provide us life, it also brings us into the present moment. Both quantum physics and spiritual teachings point to the significance of the present moment. In fact, Eckhart Tolle's *Power of Now* is one of the most transformative books when it comes to awareness and Self-Inquiry.

There are three immediate benefits to focusing on breathing:

- It brings you into the present moment.
- You become relaxed.
- It is healing.

When I was going through a stressful time, yoga was like a gift from heaven. Yoga has become a thriving industry in Western culture, particularly over the past decade, and for many good reasons. It provides flexibility, strengthens and tones the body and is a great excuse to test out cool Lululemon clothing.

In Yoga, we are taught to not ruin our practice by pushing ourselves. There's a "sweet spot" where you are doing the work, but it feels natural, and you are not overdoing it.

In nature, grass isn't "forced" to grow. Jesus said, "Consider the lilies of the field, how they grow: they neither toil nor spin." *(Matthew 6.28)*

And in business, you may recall that in Stephen Covey's *7 Habits of Highly Successful People*, he compared the corporate pressures to trying to squeeze more eggs out of the golden goose until it prematurely dies. Everyone loses.

Yoga helps release energy knots, samskaras, which are left in the body from emotional or physical trauma. For those of you who sometimes feel like a giant shoelace, yoga is very effective at opening up those knots. From an overall health standpoint, it's good to keep the mind and body in its natural relaxed state.

Unlike artificial adrenaline-boosters that we see in some business seminars and marketing presentations, where the presenter jacks up his audience into a frenzy, yoga practice is quite the opposite. Instead of creating a climax, at the very end, yoga sessions end with a five-minute "shavasana", which is full relaxation with the person spread out on the floor.

Yoga can be taught at a very early age. It's encouraging to see variations of "toddler yoga" setting the stage for counterbalancing societal pressures. You can't put a price tag on healthy, holistic practices.

Most of us pay more attention to planning a vacation or taking care of our car than we do ourselves.

A simple walk is cathartic. But even when people take walks, they're not in the moment: they're either exercising, talking to a friend on the phone, riding their bike, or listening to music.

Without a doubt, those are great ways to spend your time, but even those simple activities can get in the way of embracing the moment and having a feeling of calm.

A meditative walk allows you to focus on each step, observe your breath, and connect with your environment. For instance, I enjoy taking a stroll around Calgary's beautiful Glenmore Reservoir or Vancouver's Stanley Park. Along some of the rocky paths, I'm able to observe the trees, flowers, water, and baby ducks. I'm able to address all three components of my well-being: mind, body, and soul.

Ohmmm!

There has been a recent onslaught of scientific evidence supporting the benefits of meditation, and there are several great books on how to meditate, which we won't go over in detail here. But usually for beginners, about five to ten minutes of meditation per day is fantastic. If you're like me, when first starting out, even two minutes can feel like an eternity.

The objective is not to block off any thoughts but to watch them with awareness as you focus on your breath. It can feel unnatural, and your mind will want to fill the space with noise. Your task is not to resist or fight back. It is to accept what is passing through. There's no failure. Just gradually move back into the awareness of your surroundings and remember, observe your breath.

In a number of his books, including *You Are Here*, Thich Nhat Hanh suggests a way of focusing: when you observe your breath, you can say to yourself, "Breathing in, I know I'm breathing in. Breathing out, I know I'm breathing out."

Good vibrations

There's nothing quite like the feeling of positive vibes. We know what it's like, on a physical level, to have low energy. We feel sluggish. There's no flow.

Compassion and generosity increase your vibration level and attract you to a more favorable environment. Another way to feel and be surrounded by good vibes is to surround yourself with good people. After having a great conversation or doing something fun with someone else, you just feel a natural buzz.

"Don't Worry, Be Happy." – Bobby McFarren

Yes! Yes! Yes!

"Love nothing but that which comes to you woven in the pattern of your destiny. For what could more aptly fit your needs?" – *Marcus Aurelius*

There was a great message in Jim Carrey's movie "Yes Man". The underlying theme was just saying yes to life. You may not necessarily say yes when it comes to learning Korean or offering your wallet to a stranger, but by allowing life to work through you.

I don't mean to suggest that being happy-go-lucky no matter what is the way to live. If a person's pet dies, or if someone loses their wallet and steps on a nail on the same day and is still grinning from ear-to-ear, then that person may have bigger issues.

Bring a "yes" to what life brings. This is a great way of deepening your consciousness. There is a saying, "Trust in God, but lock your car doors." There are many decisions we make during a day, and the more present you are, the better your decisions.

Next time you're waiting in an elevator or super-market line, try being in the moment by observing your own experience.

Are you beginning to tense up? Are you more focused on getting out of there? Perhaps your mind is spinning because of all the errands you need to run. The other option, the more sane option, is to be in harmony with the environment as it is.

"Action should come out of acceptance first, not resistance. A totally different energy flow comes out this way." – Eckhart Tolle

"We don't have to struggle to be free. Absence of struggle is freedom." – Chogyam Trungpa

No matter where you go, there you are. Be there fully.

Sometimes you can change it, other times you just simply release. It's not always pleasant, but that's okay. It is part of the theatre of life designed to teach you something if you let it.

Zen Buddhists tell us not to be attached to the outcome, and just be open to whatever may happen. Flexibility is a very good attribute to have. It is similar to the wisdom of the Tao, where you are more like a palm tree, bending and swaying from side to side whenever there is a strong wind. This also gives you the gift of serendipity.

This is not just a theory, nor is it accessible to just the spiritual domain. Steve Forbes advised that one of the most important things for success is to be prepared for serendipity.

Life has an interesting way of creeping up behind you and providing a grab bag of unexpected events.

As I have discussed, our culture places a huge emphasis on happiness as another area of achievement. If you can demonstrate to the world you are happy it becomes a status symbol, or commodity, of its own.

Advertisers are good at picking up on this. At a cocktail party, while people compare themselves to others in terms of how they're dressed, their status and occupation, they are also comparing their perceived happiness to those around them.

Many spiritual teachings warn us that psyching ourselves up into thinking everything is fine only creates further misery in some form or another. I fully agree. Part of integrity is being honest with ourselves. They say if you're sad, go ahead and be sad. As an observer, watch how your body reacts. As Krishnamurti would say, "let it burn through you".

You see, we are so quick to eradicate uncomfortable emotions instead of allowing ourselves to feel and observe them. Instead, we drown the discomfort with shopping, food, drugs or alcohol in the hopes of blocking out the underlying messages. This energy has to move somewhere. Quite often, it eventually leads to a host of physical ailments. It's good practice to allow your body to release this energy organically.

Allowing

"The winds of grace are always blowing, but you have to raise the sail." – Sri Ramakrishna

"Stress doesn't exist in this world; only people thinking stressful thoughts." – Wayne Dyer

Allowing doesn't mean being passive or lethargic. In fact, allowing clears the way for a novel response instead of a conditioned one. By allowing, there is a healing process, an opening up of past wounds and releasing them. You begin to feel more buoyant as you go with the flow.

In my case, as I witnessed my own life crumble before me, "allowing" gave me the much-needed space I required to begin my own self-recovery.

As I was starting my own healing journey there were far more periods of suffering, yet at the same time, I touched on something that is difficult to describe. It was beyond thought and it came more from the heart.

Live each day as if it were your last, because one day, you'll be right. To take it a step further, try "dying before you die", as spiritual leaders have discussed. It's a concept where you assume you are probably dead. This is a way of freeing yourself from the ego. If you wipe away your job and your status, what is left?

In Steve Jobs' 2005 Stanford Commencement address, he talked about living each day as if it were your last, reminding yourself that you'll be dead soon. He warned students to avoid being trapped by dogma and following their intuition.

Being aware is not as simple as it sounds. We are too concerned about fixing problems and thinking about the future. We are so used to our own prejudices that it's difficult to break away from this pattern.

Going deeper into our minds doesn't mean thinking our way out of our mess; it means the opposite. This is part of the "allowing". Say, you go to the theater, and halfway through the movie, your body tenses up and your heartbeat quickens.

Is it because of the thriller you're watching, the hot date, or the oversized, sugary pop? Or is it all of the above? This is the beginning of what I like to refer to as "distilled thinking"—we look within before taking action.

Einstein, Newton and many other geniuses had something in common. They embraced the gaps between thinking, the gaps that come from a much vaster intelligence than from the conditioned mind. Their IQs played a part in their success, of course, but their level of insight was the catalyst in manifesting breakthrough equations.

The famous apple on the head moment happened when Newton was lying under a tree. The common denominator: space is honored between the thoughts. They oscillated between thought and not trying to have thoughts.

In this gap lies creativity. This is similar to Eckhart Tolle's message.

The BIG picture

"When you are inspired by some great purpose, some extraordinary project, all your thoughts break their bonds: Your mind transcends limitations, your consciousness expands in every direction and you find yourself in a new, great, and

wonderful world. Dormant forces, faculties and talents become alive, and you discover yourself to be a greater person by far than you ever dreamed yourself to be." – Patanjali

A great way to expand our horizons literally and figuratively is by paying closer attention not just to objects, but to space. We relate to what our limited senses tell us to relate to—our homes, the coffee cup, a squirrel. Buddhism's main teaching is about emptiness. The Tao refers to the world of 10,000 things. Both are part of the big picture.

"The most beautiful experience we can have is the mysterious. It is the fundamental emotion which stands at the cradle of true art and true science." – Einstein

It's fascinating how things begin to take shape as soon as we allow ourselves to embrace a larger part of ourselves. A transformation happens as we walk from our six-inch, black-and-white screens into the amphitheater of life. Our world takes on a bigger meaning. People who are caught up in their own problems and out of touch with the big picture tend to physically (and physiologically) manifest low vibrations.

Low vibrational people are like the man on the speeding horse. They are far more easily influenced and swayed. High vibrational energy, on the other hand, synchronizes with other sources of positive energy. The world seems a lot kinder, strangers help along the way, and unexpected opportunities present themselves. So if this makes intuitive sense, why aren't more people following this approach?

I think it's because the ego has become so powerful that it takes control of everything we do. It could also be because the promise of temporary pleasure makes us think we can attach ourselves to that artificial bliss, so we continue to follow the same pattern.

People would be astounded by how much negativity continues to guide their lives. One reason the pattern is so difficult to break is that we're so scared of what we'll find deep within ourselves. Fear may kick in because we're scared of failure or losing what we already have. It's the devil-you-know approach.

But I say meet fear head on.

When I was a kid, I had a reoccurring nightmare. I was watching a school play, but as soon as the curtain rose, a hideous creature would appear. It was a terrifying creature with multiple legs and arms, and it would jump off the stage and chase all the children in the audience. And for some reason, I was the slowest kid. The harder I tried to get away, the slower I became. As soon as this thing roared and latched onto me, I would scream and wake up.

This dream reoccurred for a few weeks until finally, while I was dreaming, I became aware that I was in a nightmare and could see myself as part of something that wasn't my true reality. After that, I eventually stopped having that dream altogether.

Check your "gut"

"People take different roads seeking fulfillment and happiness. Just because they're not on your road doesn't mean they've gotten lost." – Dalai Lama

"Once you make a decision, the universe conspires to make it happen." – Ralph Waldo Emerson

There is, of course, the traditional "gut check" which may involve loosening the belt an extra notch after beer-and-wing night at the local pub. But here, a gut check refers to intuition.

I am a strong believer in doing what you love, which means checking in with your gut. Relying more on your intuitive gut is perhaps one of the best investments you can make. This intuition is often referred to as R-brain, or EQ, or emotional quotient/intelligence.

In the business world as well as our personal lives, we have been so conditioned to focus on responding with the right answer that we miss out what is far more important—asking the right question.

Asking the right question is the basis for creativity. It no longer relegates our thinking to our limited knowledge and confines us to a linear world. When we go with our gut, it reveals our humanity. By the same token, it broadens our "receptivity" muscles, and by doing so, we become more engaged and learn to go deeper. By doing the gut-check, we can allow ourselves to derive deeper meaning from a situation instead of being reactive. The saying goes that we only use 10 percent of our brains. By opening up the portal to the non-linear world, there's infinitely more power.

Western culture predominantly focuses too much on solutions, via the left brain. When we move inward, we rely less on accumulated information, which is how most of us are used to using our brains. It is said that knowledge is power... but what kind of power are we talking about?

It certainly may help you get to the front of the class, get a promotion, or win at Trivial Pursuit, but when you really look deep within, is this the kind of power that will offer the true freedom you're looking for?

Here's another reason why it makes sense to be aware of the totality of the mind. We start shifting towards wisdom, which is far more vast than knowledge.

I am by no means suggesting that you not take good advice or appreciate an expert opinion. Just make sure you have it virus-scanned before taking appropriate action.

Another reason we may want to check with our gut is to avoid embarrassment later on. Prior to the internet, a person could do something they might regret, and the next day, it would most likely be forgotten.

Can you imagine what would happen today? You'd probably get a number of bystanders taking snapshots, and the following morning you'd be on various Facebook profiles. Decades later, when you've moved into the corporate world, a potential employer could easily Google your name and come up with a foolish moment, probably not a good first impression.

So, while you are practicing awareness, it may also help to keep in mind that others are keeping an eye out for you—maybe not for purely altruistic reasons, but as "universal guides". Remember, technology can be your friend.

Accumulation

"The man who chases two rabbits catches neither." – Confucius

For many, our lives are desperately in need of a garage sale. There is so much accumulated clutter in our lives. By letting go, we gain more, not less.

"What you resist persists." – Jung

Gratitude

Most of us understand that it is important to be grateful, although sometimes it's easier said than done. It's very easy to become caught up in our own worlds.

This is where it makes sense to practice daily gratitude; to appreciate what we have. I think it is important that gratitude be felt. There are many things to be grateful for. By the very act of reading this sentence, you can be grateful for the gift of breathing, the ability to read, and the ability to afford to purchase something as simple as this book (which just happens to be on my gratitude list as well).

Thank you. ☺

We can take a couple of minutes every night before going to bed to remind ourselves of the gratitude we feel. If you're not feeling gratitude for things many other people might be grateful for, don't worry. It's more important to be authentic. Your gratitude list can be something as simple and vital as having an appreciation for your senses, your basic faculties, your breath and just "being".

After a bit of practice, you may find you sleep more deeply and peacefully, as you think about what you're grateful for before drifting off into la-la land.

The seeds of happiness, gratitude, and awareness are fed by this simple act of giving. You don't need to save the world. Small acts like anonymously leaving behind a quarter for a stranger are enough to get the ball rolling. It will be different for everyone.

Gratitude is a wonderful way to grow the seeds of love.

"It is in giving that we receive." - Saint Francis

And Gandhi said, "The best way to find yourself is to lose yourself in the service of others."

Whatever you're looking for in life, offer it first.

Loving every minute

"To love is recognizing yourself in another." – Eckhart Tolle

Love and happiness are two prominent words used to direct us to freedom. We move into our true place of love, which is not the kind of love that is normally marketed from an egoic place, by bringing in presence. When your consciousness is there, you can really appreciate love and happiness.

Money, money, money

Here are some interesting quotes about money:

"Mo Money, Mo Problems" – Mase

"I know of nothing more despicable and pathetic than a man who devotes all the hours of the waking day to the making of money for money's sake." – John D. Rockefeller

"I have made millions, but they have brought me no happiness." – John D. Rockefeller

"Money often costs too much." – Ralph Waldo Emerson

"Whoever loves money never has money enough; whoever loves wealth is never satisfied with his income." – Ecclesiastes 5.10

Let's face it, for the majority of us, it's easier to focus on money than pretty much anything else. We strive, struggle, and may even be financially successful. If we put the entire focus on money it may take away our energy from other important aspects of our life like family. The pleasure money brings doesn't last long, and in fact, it can increase the feeling of emptiness.

"Some people are so poor, all they have is money." – Bob Marley

We are trained to believe that time = money. But I'm certain we can come up with a less limiting adage. If we base our decisions on money, how much quality time will we be able to spend with friends and family? If faced with going to our daughter's school play or getting an opportunity to work a few hours overtime, our conditioning may sway us to think the latter is the more responsible act.

Could you imagine if someone, like Warren Buffett, based his life on this formula? Taking a simple stroll to the nearby convenience store to buy a Cherry Cola, could cost him thousands of dollars. I personally believe that he is an incredible mentor to those stuck on this formula. He shows there's another way. I sense he is a person who has great integrity and moral depth.

"Money will buy you a bed, but not a good night's sleep; a house, but not a home; a companion, but not a friend." – Zig Ziglar

Many of us heard stories of lotto winners who go bankrupt and get depressed. As I'm writing this, people are clamoring for that rapidly growing Powerball lottery which just surpassed one billion dollars. As research shows, even lottery winners may end up feeling worse off than when they won.

Money is not the ticket to happiness; it's the other way around. Let's face it, as we've talked about in great detail, people are poor predictors of happiness. Their happiness is similar to horse racing. You could have all the seemingly reliable predictors of happiness, but in the long run, you fall short.

Besides, if the best things in life are free and the second best are quite expensive, wouldn't it make sense economically and mentally to focus more on the first?

It's all relative

If you really think about it, people tend to be more concerned with relative than absolute happiness. H.L. Menken's definition of wealth is a situation in which a person makes $100/year more than his wife's sister's husband.

I believe there is something inherently flawed in this approach. It's rooted in ego, which can't be a good thing. This concept of relative wealth not only applies to bank accounts, but also to something as intangible as spirituality. This is another crafty ego trap, in which people who can't catch up financially decide they may as well carve a niche for themselves in the spiritual domain, where admission is free and enlightenment doesn't cost much more.

Speaking of economics, there is a powerful concept that's worth remembering—the law of diminishing returns. This illustrates how each incremental unit we add of pretty much anything (whether it be money, sex, food), the more those units decrease in value.

"The least of things with a meaning is worth more in life than the greatest of things without it." – Carl Jung

My first car was a '79 Datsun beater when I was eighteen. I treated this object like a mother would treat her newborn. All I needed was four wheels. No more spending hours transferring from bus to bus. It was probably close to the feeling Jefferson had when signing the Declaration of Independence.

After a while I traded up with the help of my father and got a VW convertible. Again, I was in bliss. Eventually, as I kept trading up, I never quite felt the same level joy as I did with those first cars.

The same thing happened when I went to Vegas with my brother, Kav. The first time we went, I thought I died and went to heaven. The second time, which was several years later, we stayed in a penthouse suite at Caesars Palace instead of Motel 6 and had exceptional VIP treatment. It was tons of fun, but it wasn't as fun as that first time.

What's our highest currency?

Money is actually a good thing in itself. It raises the standard of living. And it's a lot more convenient than bartering. But if you're motivated by the accumulation of it, by thinking it's going to raise your level of happiness, studies show this may not be the case.

"I spent a lot of money on booze, birds, and fast cars. The rest I just squandered." – George Best

There is a way to have your cake and eat it, too. There are also several examples of people who put money to good use. It might come as no surprise, but Bill Gates and Warren Buffett spring to mind. Two of the world's richest individuals are also very generous. Buffett gave away 85 percent of his fortune to the Gates Foundation.

I also think there's no coincidence that both Gates and Buffett appear genuinely happy and down to earth.

"Use me, God. Show me how to take who I am, who I want to be, and what I can do, and use it for a purpose greater than myself." – Martin Luther King Jr.

Money, therefore, is not a bad thing. It's just imperative that we align our definitions of wealth to not be motivated by greed, fame, or power. It is important to recognize that true happiness cannot be bought. Once this truth is realized, it lifts a tremendous burden, allowing us to focus on our principles.

"Lots of people want to ride with you in the limo, but what you want is someone who will take the bus with you when the limo breaks down." – Oprah Winfrey

While on the topic of dollars, Benjamin Franklin is a great example of someone who wanted to be of service. Not only was he a hardcore philanthropist, despite all his inventions, he never patented a thing. This is practically unheard of especially in today's environment where everyone is guarded and overprotective.

"I look at the inner scorecard." – Warren Buffett

"If you make money your god, it will plague you like the devil." – Henry Fielding

"That don't impress me much." – Shania Twain

Rather than impress—connect. Remember that the true currency in life is pure happiness.

Constant cravings

Advertisers recognize we're slaves to our cravings. There are a number of effective ads that start off with a phrase like, "Satisfy your cravings". Then they will juxtapose it with a picture of a tantalizing burger or bright sports car. When we chase our cravings, we miss out on something far greater.

Songs like the Rolling Stones, "Can't Get No Satisfaction", remind us to pause. There are no shortages of temptation, most of which distract us from our true purpose. We are missing the point of our journey. These are part of Buddhist teachings.

We must decide between stimulus and response. To recognize this on a deeper level takes practice. Most of us aren't in the habit of "checking in" with ourselves, thus it becomes easy to get sucked into the vortex of other distractions.

The more we practice becoming aware of our feelings and pay attention to them, the better we are able to know whether we're tempted by our cravings or not. One of the many benefits of awareness is that it's an effective way to diminish our cravings—to help us focus on our presence.

Nature or nurture

Here's one of those major topics discussed in psychology classes. I remember learning about how genes determine our behavior to a large extent. Through the whole nature-nurture debate, there was compelling evidence on the 'nature' side suggesting how much genes play a role. Even twins who were born and lived separate lives were shown to develop very similar tastes. Research has also shown this to be true when it comes to what is a "baseline" of happiness.

But nurture also plays a role. In a 1996 interview with the Chicago Tribune, columnist Ann Landers said, "I owe a lot to my parents and to my Iowa heritage. I think middle-class American values have helped me tremendously—the principles, the morality."

In his book, *Outliers*, Malcolm Gladwell starts off by emphasizing the impact that community has on one's longevity, health, and happiness.

These cases show how both nature and nurture are strong determinants.

We could leave it at that. But something more is involved. Every individual has the ability to access his true self. Regardless of your background, your health or economic circumstances, every living being has the ability to truly know themselves.

Those who have been ostensibly lucky in life can only be lucky to a point. When one feels a degree of safety and comfort, there is less likelihood of moving past their day-to-day routine.

Conversely, as with lotto winners or cancer victims, although there is a temporary emotional event, over a period of time, these individuals return back to their same or better level of happiness. Both of these examples illustrate that our happiness tends to waver around our own predisposed level.

Additionally, the ones who have been "forced into" drastic life circumstances have an opportunity to move deeper within, to find out what they are made of, and to access happiness.

You are not just living your life. You ARE life.

Remember the Jacksons?

Spirituality can be as simple as A-B-C.

A—Attention

To simply hear the word, ATTENTION, brings you immediately to the present. All distractions and agitations are pulled back with no effort or strain. If you are able to do that for 5 seconds, it is already a great step. Attention heightens your senses. Attention drops thinking, suspends ego and aligns you with Source. Joy, peace, love and happiness are given the green light for grace to come through. More attention means more YOU.

B—Breathe

To maintain this alert presence, breathing is your friend. Observing your breath is one of the constant reminders in Yoga. Some practices suggest holding your breath for a certain count or saying a mantra but this is not a requirement. You can just enjoy the quality of your breath. It will allow you to focus even deeper into it. Are they short breaths? Are they deep breaths? Are the breaths cold or warm? Do you smell your surroundings like a nearby flower or a juicy pizza? The more we bring attention to our breathing, the more the breaths will begin to deepen on their own. You are merely riding the breath rather than controlling the breath.

C—Clearance

Clearance is where we do a body scan; we perceive and sense our bodies top to bottom, and bottom to top, slowly feeling sensations. This can be done a few times. Do you notice any energy knots as you scan through? If so, bring more focus to those areas, accept the sensations and allow for any release of energy knots. This complements both your spirituality and your happiness.

Oh, and don't forget to SMILE :-)

After reading this book, readers will hopefully relate to the "smile" from a conscious level. We may recall smiling with a social mask doesn't help to transcend to pure happiness. There have been countless articles and sales manuals on the importance of smiling.

Smiling at people from your heart makes them feel better about themselves, and helps you feel better on a deeper level. Smiling sends a message that we're warm, helpful, friendly people. If we're books, smiling is our cover. Smiling authentically creates our true cover, and we don't want to blow our cover.

About the Author

Life was going well. THEN IT HAPPENED. On September 13, 2013, I was admitted to Vancouver General Hospital with a brain tumor which, according to the surgeon, was the largest he had operated on to date.

With what little consciousness I had after the operation, they took me back for an MRI. I barely remember hearing, "Don't move!" I had lost sense of what was happening. Moments later, I recalled a shout, "Don't move!"

Then I recalled someone saying I was bleeding. I thought I was back in surgery. After that point, I heard the rollers from the operating room again. I heard someone say, "Clearance!" Then I jumped, then again. It felt as if I was dying on the spot, but I didn't see a bright light. I didn't think my Spirit had left.

After, it was told to me that although I was brought back for the MRI, the second surgery that day never happened, although the dreams seemed very real.

The brain cancer, grade three, required chemo and radiation. The size and location of the disease within my brain left me with significant permanent problems. My thinking and memory have been affected and I have difficulty telling time. I have lost 50% vision in each eye. This has introduced limitations to previously valued activities like driving, playing chess and running. Fortunately, my cane allows me to be somewhat mobile.

I have problems reading and understanding words, including simple words and numbers. My reading ability has, for the most part, been taken away. As a voracious reader, this was challenging for me to accept. What might seem surprising is how the disease affected my writing abilities. I can comfortably type or write a thought, but if I come back to see what I have written, it's very difficult to read.

Through this, however, I still believe that inner freedom is not just a gift for a privileged few. It's accessible to everyone.

The remarkable compassion, love and support from close family and friends, pulled me through this challenging period in my life. Nurses, doctors, teachers, and other practitioners remind us of our higher calling. The seeds of empathy open up to kindness and compassion.

Having helped others find joy in life in my work as a happiness coach, I was now personally faced with disabilities beyond anything I had imagined.

Paradoxically, I had to become my own student.

A positive attitude and willpower may help in some situations, but mine felt so complex and overwhelming that it required a different approach and a deeper investigation.

As a society, we tend to be driven by work, rushing from one thing to the next. Sometimes it is helpful to engage qualities such as stillness, acceptance, empathy and compassion, for ourselves and others, in order to find meaning in life's challenges and to discover who we really are. This deep introspection has helped me find my path to a new real life adventure.

Currently, I am grateful to be a cancer survivor. I enjoy spreading the word of happiness and spirituality to many gatherings, companies and people who are interested in improving their lives.

This includes running workshops, giving lectures, helping businesses and working with media. I facilitate the Eckhart Tolle group in Vancouver and have been a guest on radio shows and TV.

I have also spoken to universities and have most recently been the keynote speaker at the Canadian Cancer Society in Vancouver.

Acknowledgements

This book took several years to complete. Surgery presented many challenges that needed to be overcome before I could continue my writing.

This book would not have been possible without the support of incredible friends and family.

Special thanks go out to my father, Reze, and my mother, Pari, who have constantly encouraged me. I am so grateful for my amazing brother, Kav, who has always "believed in me". I feel so blessed to have you for my family.

I would like to thank Cathy "Angel" and Neil Schlosser for their help throughout this book process and for their ongoing support. Their time and energy are much appreciated.

Many thanks go to Dr. Kaiyo Nedd, who helped me through surgery and gave me genuine care and friendship.

I am also grateful to Franchesco and Reet, Reg and Kisch Neufeld, Steve and Diane Valetta, the Naddafs, Guity and Mehdi Adib, and the Canadian Cancer Society for helping me extend this message to others who could use the support.

Feel free to contact the author for a presentation, to order books or any other information:

Bob Molavi, FMA, BA Econ
Happiness Coach

bob@purehappinesscoach.com
www.purehappinesscoach.com

Facebook: Bob Molavi / LinkedIn: Bob Molavi